Extreme Longevity

Additional Publications from Michael Ten

Radical Life Extension: Psychological, Metaphysical, and Political Implications

Attempt to Utilize Cryonics (Second Edition): Reasons Why Utilizing Human Cryopreservation Is Ultimately Desirable

Outlaw Psychiatric Slavery (First Edition): Reasons for Outlawing Civil Commitment and the Insanity Defense

Extreme Longevity

Using Social Media to Spark
a Life Extension Revolution

Michael Ten

Extreme Longevity

Using Social Media to Spark a Life Extension Revolution

ISBN-13: 978-1535528559

ISBN-10: 1535528559

Websites
MichaelTen.com

Twitter
@iMichaelTen

Facebook
Facebook.com/tenmichael

Email
hello@MichaelTen.com

Acknowledgements and Dedications

I appreciate all those who have guided me in authentically beneficial ways and those who have motivated me to create more goodness and peace on Earth.

I appreciate all family, friends, and others that have helped me in many various ways.

This book is dedicated to all humans who strive to live lives of authentic decency and authentic peace.

Table of Contents

Preface

In this book I am attempting to explain in significant detail how we can hasten the defeat of aging using social media.

For every day by which we hasten the defeat of aging, we save 100,000 lives. For every year by which we hasten the defeat of aging, we save 36,500,000 lives. Do not forget this. I could wait longer to publish this book. This book is not perfect, but I think it is better to release information often. Nothing will be perfect.

This book is about hastening the defeat of aging and sparking a war against aging. Thank you in advance for reading it.

I hope this book is pleasurable and of value to you. I mean that sincerely.

Introduction

This short book is about life extension. It is about radical life extension. I want to empower you and more. I want to help show you how social media can be harnessed to help hasten the defeat of aging.

I am attempting to lay forth a framework for less scientific individuals to follow in order to help hasten the defeat of aging.

Increased funding for research related to radical life extension can help propel the science forward.

I want this book to be a positive and optimistic book.

I am hoping to help spark a war against aging. I am hoping to spark a longevity revolution.

I hope to see it become common for lay individuals to advocate for the defeat of aging.

I want to empower you with knowledge about how you can help to hasten the defeat of aging.

More funds are need for early stage research related to regenerative medicine and extreme longevity. These funds can come from public government funds and/or millions of individuals who want to see aging defeated.

Aging will not defeat itself.

I hope to encourage young adults to study biogerontology.

I hope to raise awareness for a revolution related to the defeat of aging so that we can have politicians and lay people support the defeat of aging.

Eventually, this may culminate in lawmakers/politicians voting in legislatures to dramatically increase funding related to programs that may defeat aging.

Additionally, this may culminate in lay people donating to organizations like SENS Research Foundation, Buck Institute, and Methuselah Foundation.

This is how I hope as a non-biologist to help hasten the defeat of aging.

Tragedy of Aging

Is there anything more tragic than the sheer number of deaths caused by human aging? Nothing is more tragic than human aging.

I first purchased the book Ending Aging in about 2009.

Aubrey de Grey, in the book Ending Aging, describes the ethical argument that if you could do one thing to do the most good, it would be to defeat aging and increase the amount of healthy years that humans live.

Ultimately, there is nothing more tragic than aging. Nothing comes close to aging with regards to the scale at which death is created.

We need more individuals on social media proclaiming that they want to see aging defeated.

If enough individuals demand that aging is defeated, then public dollars for research related to the defeat of aging will materialize.

The tragedy of aging is why I am writing this book.

The Science of It

I want to briefly talk about the science related to defeating aging.

I am not a biogerontologist.

You can read the book Ending Aging: The Rejuvenation Breakthroughs That Could Reverse Human Aging in Our Lifetime by Aubrey de Grey to learn about the details of how aging might be defeated. I hope that you have read this book, and I hope that you do read it if you have not already read it.

There are seven main types of bodily damage caused by aging.

The theory behind strategies for negligible engineered senescence is that if we can repair the seven types of damage that occur in human cells, then humans could potentially live indefinitely.

The aforementioned book goes into great detail as to about how this might actually be accomplished.

Goals

There are four main goals of this book.

The first is to help increase donations to organization such as SENS Research Foundation, Methuselah Foundation, Buck Institute for Research on Aging, and similar organizations. I also hope to help build awareness for these organizations through social media.

The second goal is to help build awareness through increased media coverage of longevity research. This can be done through contacting media organizations and requesting that they cover stories related to longevity, radical life extension, cryonics, and so forth.

The third goal is to help increase public funding for longevity research and organizations like the aforementioned. This can be accomplished through contact law makers through social media, email, and so forth.

The fourth goal of this book is to encourage more young adults to study topics related to longevity. I hope that I can inspire young adults to pursue a career that can help to lead to an Earth on which aging does not cause so much death.

Public awareness of longevity research will grow if more individuals engage on social media. This book is about how social media and electronic communications can be used to accomplish the aforementioned.

It is possible to contact media outlets and request that they cover longevity research and radical life extension research.

It is possible to contact law makers to request that they increase funding for longevity and anti-aging research.

It is possible, using social media, to engage the public to build awareness for anti-aging and longevity research.

We must see the defeat of aging. We can accelerate the progress at which the defeat of aging happens if social media and email are effectively harnessed and utilized.

It is possible to inspire young adults to study topics related to longevity and biomedical gerontology.

Increasing Donations and Awareness

I want to see an increase in the amount of private donations to organizations that are helping to bring about a defeat of aging.

I want to see an increase in awareness for organizations that are devoted to bringing about the defeat of aging. This can be accomplished through communications on social media, and communications with journalists and influencers.

Increasing News Coverage

I want to see more news coverage related to topics surrounding the defeat of aging.

Increased news coverage can help to increase public awareness for topics related to the defeat of aging.

Public Funding

A major goal of this book is to eventually see individuals donating money in mass to organizations that may help to hasten the defeat of aging.

Another major goal of this book is to see individuals demanding that more public dollars are donated to research that may help to bring about a defeat of aging.

I want to see private donations to life extension research increase.

I also want to see public money available to research related to defeating aging increase.

There are quite a few ways to influence the politics of funding related to radical life extension

Few politicians are actively vocal about longevity research. This is quite unfortunate.

We need elected officials to support defeating aging. Once the general public supports defeating aging, elected officials will follow.

Politics can be a powerful force.

Politicians at all levels of government can support defeating aging.

Tweet to politicians. Email politicians. Tell them that you want to see aging defeated. Tell them that you want to see funding for longevity research increased.

Studying Biomedical Gerontology

I hope that this book will encourage young adults to study biogerontology.

I already went to school for six years after high school.

Had I read Ending Aging in high school, then I might have become a biogerontologist.

I studied psychology though. I did not study biogerontology.

It has crossed my mind to go back to school.

However, I am hoping to contribute to the field of biogerontology through helping there to be increased funding, and also to potentially encourage young adults to go into the field.

Contacting News Organization

Contacting news organizations and requesting that they cover topics related to longevity is one way we can work towards sparking an anti-aging revolution.

It will be good if more news organizations cover topics related to longevity and radical life extension.

The following is an example of a letter that may help to increase awareness of longevity related topics. Feel free to copy the letter or to modify it and to send it to organizations that you think might be interested in increasing the amount of coverage that they give to longevity and radical life extension topics.

I sent the following short letter to Science Friday, a show on National Public Radio.

Have you seen or heard science articles, videos, radio shows, pod-casts, and so forth related to longevity?

Consider contacting your favorite news organization (or just anyone you like decently) and request that they feature content related to extreme longevity.

I just contact Science Friday which appears on NPR. I've heard all sorts of shows about various science topics, but none about extreme longevity.

Here is the short request I sent them.

I went to www.sciencefriday.com/about/contact-us in order to contact Science Friday. I hope you contact a different news organization, YouTube channel, audio cast, or publication of your choosing.

Hello,

Please feature content related to extremely longevity, cryonics, regenerative medicine, and radical life extension.

Please feature organizations such as The Buck Institute for Research on Aging, SENS Research Foundation, Alcor Life Extension Foundation, Human Longevity Inc., and/or Methuselah Foundation. Please feature leaders of the some of the aforementioned organizations such as David Sinclair, Aubrey de Grey, Max Moore, and/or Brian K. Kennedy.

These topics and some of these individuals have been in the news recently and have the potential to be of interest to large numbers of individuals. This is all of interest to me as well.

Thank you.

Sincerely,

[My Name]

What news organization will you contact? If even 1,000 individuals here, out of the over 4,200 subscribers here, contact 500 different news organizations, this could help to increase interest and awareness about radical life extension and longevity significantly.

I am interested in hearing more in the media about extreme longevity, cryonics, and radical life extension. Are you?

Social Media

Social media can be harnessed to help defeat aging. Many individuals can come together to spread worthwhile messages related to defeating aging.

Social media can be used as a tool for social change.

This section of the book is how to mobilize social media to defeat aging.

Twitter, Reddit, Facebook, YouTube and so forth can all be mobilized to leverage social connections.

Social media platforms can be utilized to help hasten the defeat of aging. Social media can be tremendously powerful.

You can Tweet to tell others that you support the defeat of aging. You can write a Tumblr post stating that you want aging to be defeated.

You can write and publish an article about why you want to see aging defeated. There is no shortage of options on how you can voice your support for the defeat of aging over social media.

Twitter

There are many ways to utilize Twitter to help hasten the defeat of aging. Every little bit of effort helps. Do not spam, but be persistent in your efforts. Attempt to contribute in a valuable way to social media spheres.

At least once per week Tweet something like, "Donate to SENS Research Foundation http://sens.org/Donate #NotProAging #DefeatAging #SENS @senstweet @aubreydegrey @LifespanIO" Use Buffer.com to queue it up.

Tweet to lawmakers and journalists. Be vocal and do not spam.

When I see lawmakers on Twitter, I sometimes Tweet to them to let them know that I want to see them helping to defeat aging.

Do you follow journalists on Twitter? Tweet to them and request that they cover life extension topics.

The following is a sample Tweet (feel free to use this or modify it. "@[JournalistsTwitterHandle] Please consider covering SENS research or radical life extension. Thank you. @mfoundation @senstweet @LifespanIO @aubreydegrey"

Here is another example, to news editors and journalists, you can Tweet something like the following. Feel free to copy or modify my Tweet.

"@[JournalistsTwitterHandle] I hope [paper's name] covers organizations like @senstweet @mfoundation @LifespanIO @humanlongevity and so forth. #DefeatAging #SENS"

Here are a few more examples of Tweets that you can use or modify.

"@[JournalistsTwitterHandle] Plz write about longevity and/or SENS research. @senstweet @mfoundation @humanlongevity @LifespanIO #longevity #NotProAging"

To a representative I Tweeted the following. Please feel free to use or adapt the Tweet.

"@[CongressmansTwitterHandle] All Representatives should support defeating aging. #DefeatAging #SENS #NotProAging"

To President Obama and other congressmen, I Tweeted the following.

"@POTUS @SenSanders @SenWarren @RonWyden @MikeCrapo Politicians should support defeating aging. @senstweet @LifespanIO @BuckInstitute #SENS"

To a governor I tweeted the following.

"@JohnKasich All Governors should support increased funding for longevity research. @mfoundation @senstweet @LifespanIO #NotProAging #SENS"

To a Senator I Tweeted the following.

"@SenatorTomUdall All Senators should support life extension research. @LifespanIO @mfoundation @senstweet @SenSanders #DefeatAging #SENS"

I am not trying to be overly repetitive here. I am trying to get across the point that you can Tweet to influential individuals to help spread the word about SENS research, longevity research, and the potential to defeat aging.

Please feel free to use, and ideally adapt any or all of the previously mentioned Tweets.

If you Tweet like this someone will see the Tweets. If enough individuals Tweet with longevity related hashtags, then they will become trending topics on Twitter, thereby gaining more exposure.

Using Buffer
Use Buffer.com to promote defeating aging on social media!

Buffer allows you to schedule Tweets, Facebook posts, Google+ posts, LinkedIn posts and so forth. You can schedule about 10 postings for free. Once you create them you can schedule how often they are published. I recommend that you try using Buffer to spread the word about defeating aging. I set buffer to publish a Tweet, Facebook post, and Google Plus post once per day. You can experiment to see what works best for you.

Hashtags

There are quite a few ways to utilize social media. Hashtags are one way of utilizing and organizing social media.

Hashtags can be used on Facebook, Vine, Twitter, Tumblr, and also on other social media sites.

Here is a list of hashtags that can be used to mobilize and organize support for defeating aging over social media.

> #DefeatAging
> #NotProAging
> #Longevity
> #SENSResearch
> #SENS
> #RadicalLifeExtension
> #ExtremeLongevity
> #AntiAging
> #LifeExtension
> #Health

This list is a short list of hashtags. Hashtags should be dynamic. Create your own hashtags! Be creative.

If enough grassroots support for defeating aging is created, then hashtags related to the defeat of aging may become trending on Twitter.

If more individuals use these hashtags on social media, the more awareness can be built about radical life extension technologies.

Reddit

Reddit can be utilized to coordinate grassroots activism on Reddit.

Sub-Reddits directly related to longevity and radical life extension are as follows.

> www.reddit.com/r/longevity
> www.reddit.com/r/sens
> www.reddit.com/r/GrassrootsLongevity

Sub-Reddits indirectly related to longevity and radical life extension.

> www.reddit.com/r/transhuman
> www.reddit.com/r/transhumanism
> www.reddit.com/r/singularity

YouTube

YouTube can be used as a social media site. Recently I have seen efforts to contact prominent YouTube publishers with the suggestion that they create videos about topics related to longevity, anti-aging, and radical life extension.

You can create your own videos related to radical life extension and publish them on YouTube. You can also send messages on YouTube to your favorite video creators suggesting that they create videos related to radical life extension, SENS research, longevity, and so forth.

YouTube can probably be leveraged as a platform to hasten the defeat of aging a lot more than it currently is.

Thunderclap

Thunderclap (www.thunderclap.it) is a relatively new platform for spreading the word about ideas via social media.

It is sort of like a Kickstarter for social media campaigns.

I have recently started a Thunderclap for hastening the defeat of aging. It will probably not succeed. As of this writing I have started two Thunderclap campaigns. Both have failed.

I would encourage you to utilize Thunderclap, hopefully successfully, to help hasten the defeat of aging.

Someone with a good social media reach may be able to start a successful Thunderclap related to defeating aging.

I am confident that Thunderclap can eventually be utilized successfully to help hasten the defeat of aging.

Conclusion

There are a multitude of social networks. They can all potentially be leveraged to spread messages that support the defeat of aging.

Weather you use Tumblr, Twitter, Facebook, Vine, YouTube, or so forth, you can utilize the social media platform to help hasten the defeat of aging.

I hope that you use your own creativity to take these ideas here related to social media, and to build upon them and extend them.

Cryonics

Cryonics is worth discussing. Cryonics is a metaphorical ambulance to the future.

Cryonics is what happens when someone, after legal death, undergoes a procedure to have their body and sometimes just head or brain brought to an extremely cold temperature so as to preserve it. The hope is that the individual can potentially be revived at a future date when technology progress far enough.

I hope that all individuals who want to are able to undergo cryonics procedures.

Cryonics should eventually be publicly funded if economically possible. From an ethical perspective, all individuals who want to utilize cryonics should be able to do so if economically possible.

Social media can be utilized to build awareness about cryonics technologies.

For more information about cryonics, please consider reading the book that I wrote, Attempt to Utilize Cryonics (Second Edition): Why Utilizing Human Cryopreservation Is Ultimately Desirable.

Conclusion

Thank you for reading this relatively short book. I hope that you now have ideas about what you can do to help hasten the defeat of aging. A revolution to defeat aging is necessary.

Nothing is more tragic than aging. Social media is a powerful tool. We can leverage its advantages in order to help hasten the defeat of aging.

If many individuals put form concerted effort, we can probably defeat aging sooner than we might think.

Support institutions like Buck Institute, Methuselah Foundation, and SENS Research Foundation. Do what you can to help hasten the defeat of aging.

This book is meant to help empower you. I want to empower you, so that you can empower others. This book is a starting point.

If you write and publish another book about this same topic, that expands on these ideas, I will be quite happy. I want to see aging defeated.

We can help to increase funding for organizations that will hasten the defeat of aging.

We can increase public funding for longevity organizations through contact law makers.

We can increase the amount of media coverage that longevity related organizations receive by contacting media professionals and influencers.

We can inspire young adults to pursue careers that may lead to the defeat of aging.

All of this is possible. All of this is worthwhile.

Be persistent with social media. It can sometimes take a while for a worthwhile message to gain traction. Do not give up in your efforts to spread the word about radical life extension.

Thank you for reading this book. I hope you leave an honest review of it where you can. I hope that you work to spread the word about research which may lead to the eventual defeat of aging.

Book Recommendations

Ending Aging: The Rejuvenation Breakthroughs That Could Reverse Human Aging in Our Lifetime
by Aubrey de Grey and Michael Rae

Abundance: The Future Is Better Than You Think
by Peter H. Diamandis and Steven Kotler

The Art of Non-Conformity: Set Your Own Rules, Live the Life You Want, and Change the World
by Chris Guillebeau

The Art of Peace
by John Stevens and Morihei Ueshiba

Fatal Freedom: The Ethics and Politics of Suicide
by Thomas Szasz

Suicide Prohibition: The Shame of Medicine
by Thomas Szasz

Afterword

Thank you for reading this book. I hope that this book has provided you with ideas about how you can help to hasten the defeat of aging.

Please leave an honest review of this book where you are able to.

Additionally, please sign up for my mailing list so that you can stay up to date on when I release future books. You can sign up for the mailing list at www.MichaelTen.com/Subscribe or just visit my website at www.MichaelTen.com.